# Making Baskets

## by Maryanne Gillooly

Basketry, the oldest craft known to mankind, has evolved into an art as basket weavers grow more creative in both design and choice of materials. We see baskets that are pleated and plaited, curled and twisted, beaded and braided.

Try it yourself. By following the directions in this bulletin, you can create two beautiful, functional baskets — a 10-inch melon-shaped basket and a 10-inch egg-shaped basket. More important, you'll understand the basics of basket-weaving and be ready to introduce your own ideas into your next basket — your own special design, colors, and "wild" materials.

You'll be surprised how quickly you can weave these baskets, and how inexpensive the materials are. Count on about 5 hours to complete one basket, and an average of $7 for materials if you buy enough to weave several.

A list of sources of supplies, tools, and basket-making kits will be found at the end of this bulletin.

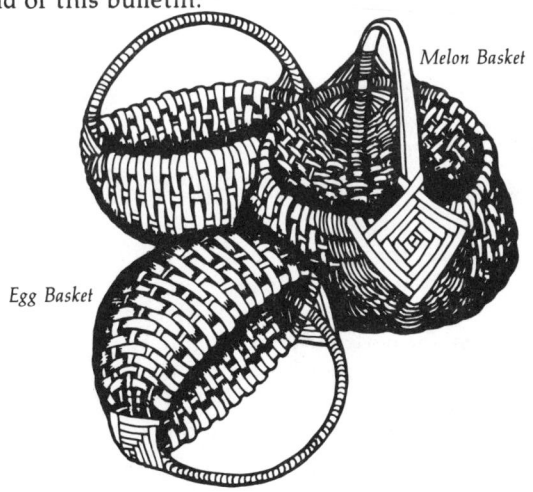

## TOOLS AND MATERIALS

### Tools

Fine sandpaper  
Tape  
Pencil  
Tape measure  
Bucket or dishpan (for soaking the reed  
Scissors  

Awl  
Pencil sharpener  
Spring-type clothespins  
Towel  
Clippers or snips  

### Materials

2 basket hoops, 10-inch size (¾-inch wide)*  
1 bundle #7 round reed (for spokes)**  
1 bundle 3/16-inch flat reed (for lashing)  
1 bundle ¼-inch flat reed (for weaving)  

* The amount of reed you buy, a 1-pound bundle, will make three 10-inch baskets, so you may want to purchase four extra hoops to make two extra baskets. Half-inch wide hoops can also be bought.
** The millimeter size on round reed varies from company to company, so check when ordering. This #7 round reed is 5 MM size. The size is listed in millimeters in the catalogs.

## DEFINITION OF TERMS

**Handle,** the top portion of the vertical hoop.  
**Handle bottom,** the bottom portion of the vertical hoop.  
**Lashing,** the weaving used to bind the two hoops together.  
**Rim,** the horizontal hoop that forms the edge of the basket.  
**Spokes,** the round reeds that form the framework of the basket and provide the warp to weave over and under.  
**Weaver,** the piece or reed or other material used to weave.

# Melon Baskets

## Step 1. Hoops

Start with the two 10-inch hoops. Sand them with fine paper if their edges are rough. Put one pencil mark on the outside of one hoop. Measure half-way around the hoop, about 16 inches, and mark the halfway point. Measure and mark two similar points on the other hoop.

Select a side of one hoop that has no seams or marks and mark it with a piece of tape. This will be the handle. Place this handle hoop on the outside of the other hoop, and have them meet at the pencil marks.

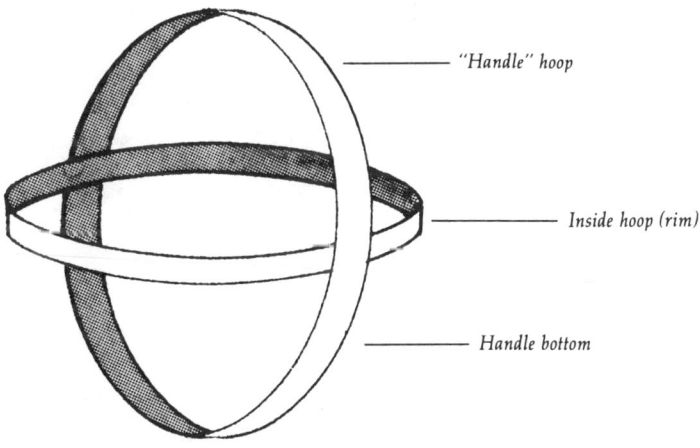

"Handle" hoop

Inside hoop (rim)

Handle bottom

## Step 2. Four-fold Lashing

The next step is to weave the four-fold lashing that will bind the two hoops together and serve as a place for the ends of the spokes to rest.

The 3/16-inch reed that you use, like other reeds, has a right, or smooth side, and a wrong, or rough side. If you bend one end back and forth you can quickly identify the splintery side and the smoother right side.

Select one of the longest pieces of 3/16-inch reed. Place it in a pan of lukewarm water. When the reed is pliable (this takes about 3 minutes), remove it and shake off any excess water.

Place the crossed hoops in front of you, making certain that the hoops are even on the pencil marks. Start with one crossed section facing you, with the taped handle on top. Follow closely the instructions and the steps below.

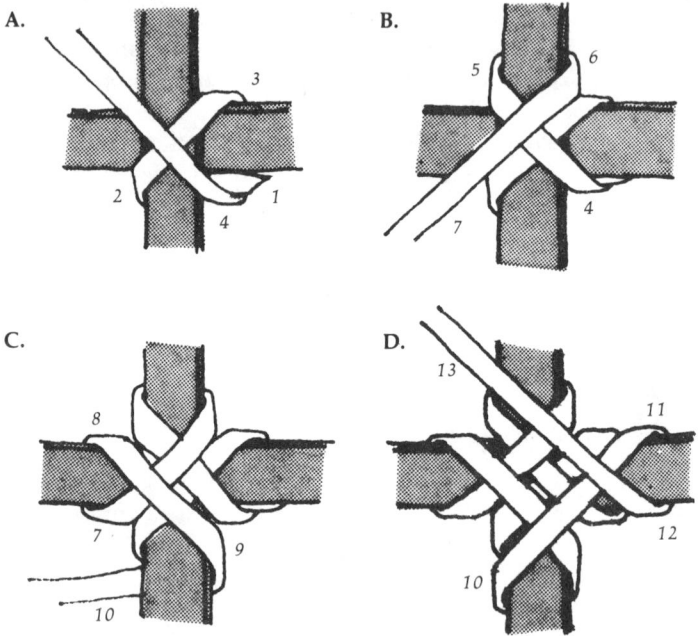

**Step A.** Place the soaked piece of reed behind the handle bottom at point 1 with the wrong side against the back of the handle bottom. Leave about an inch of the end to be tucked into the weaving as the lashing progresses. From point 2, bring the reed up and across to point 3, with the right side showing, then straight down and behind the rim to point 4.

**Step B.** Picking up at point 4, bring the reed up and across to point 5, then behind the handle to point 6. You have now formed an X across the hoops. Keeping the reed next to the previous row, bring the reed down and across to point 7.

4/MAKING BASKETS

**Step C.** Picking up at point 7, bring the reed straight up and behind the rim to point 8, then down and across to point 9. Now bring the reed behind the handle bottom to point 10.

**Step D.** Picking up at point 10, bring the reed up and across to point 11, then straight down and behind the rim to point 12. Bring the reed up and across to point 13.

At this point you can see the diamond shape of the four-fold lashing. Continue the pattern for eight rows. They can be counted on the back, behind the lashing. Make each row snug to the previous one. There will be a slight overlap on the front of the lashing.

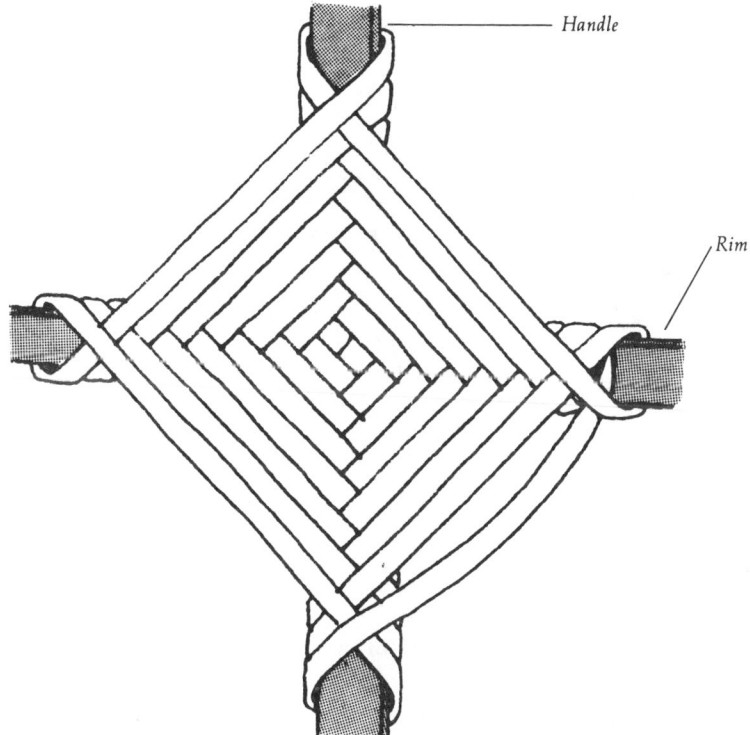

To finish the lashing, cut the end at an angle, with the scissors, then slide the reed under the last row at one of the corners. Use the awl or the pointed end of the scissors to tuck the end in firmly behind the lashing and the hoop.

Repeat this lashing on the other side. Double-check that the hoops are even on the pencil marks.

## Step 3. Spokes

The spokes form the basic structure and shape of the basket, in this case the round or "melon" shape.

Cut ten pieces of #7 round reed 15½ inches long. Sharpen both ends of each spoke with a pencil sharpener. Soak these only if they are so crooked that they will not form rounded arcs.

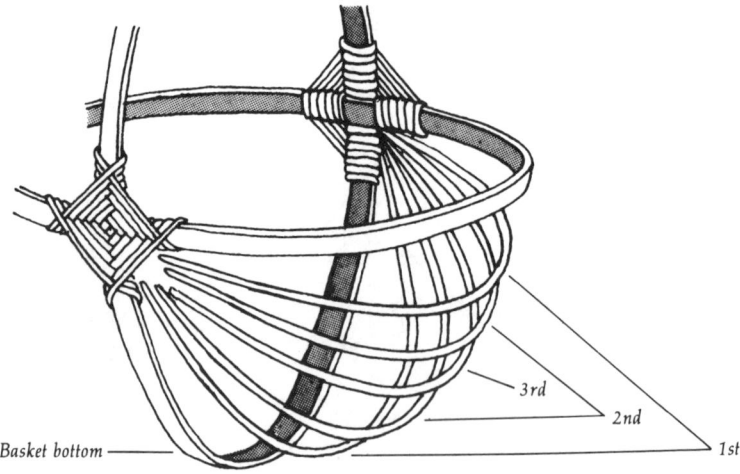

Place five spokes on one side of the basket bottom, tucking the pointed ends inside the pocket formed by the four-fold lashing. First place the two spokes nearest the rim and the bottom of the handle. Then place two more, one next to the top spoke and the other next to the bottom one. Finally, place the fifth spoke in the middle.

Repeat the placement of the spokes on the other side of the basket bottom.

## Step 4. Weaving

You now have the basic form or framework of the basket. The two hoops are firmly joined by the four-fold lashing and the spokes are evenly spaced and firmly in place.

The weaving begins at the base of the lashing and proceeds from one side of the rim to the other. You might expect that weaving would be continuous, starting at the base of one lashing and continuing under the framework until you have reached the lashing on the other side. But that isn't the way it is done. Instead, when the first piece of reed is completely woven in, you begin weaving at the base of the lashing on the other side. The weaving alternates from one side of the basket to the other as each weaver, or piece of reed, is used up, until, at the bottom of the basket, the framework is completely filled in with weaving.

The weaving is done in a simple over-one, under-one pattern. However, in the beginning, there isn't enough space between the spokes to weave in and out. So you will notice that the directions call for several steps to follow until eventually, as you continue to weave toward the center of the basket, there is enough space to weave through each spoke. This process is called breaking down. Study the diagrams and follow the instructions exactly, and you will have no trouble with it.

A.

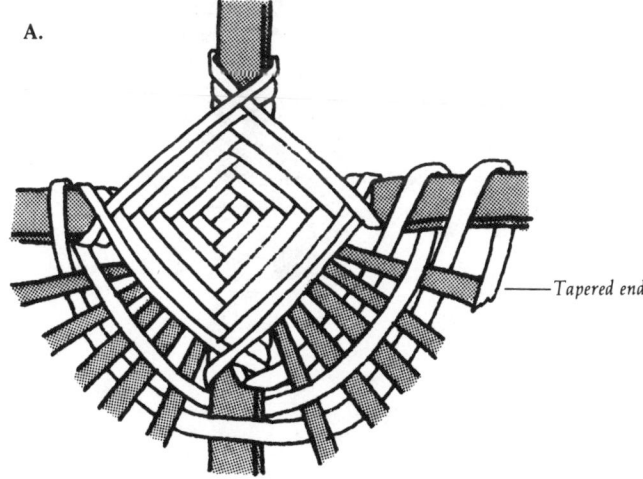

Tapered end

Before beginning to weave, soak a piece of ¼-inch reed in lukewarm water until it is pliable. This, too, takes about three minutes. It will fray and crack if soaked too long. Taper one end of the reed by cutting it diagonally with the scissors.

With the lashing on one side facing you, tuck the tapered end into the space at the bottom of the lashing, with the right side down.

Fold the reed to the right, so the right side is up. Weave it under all five spokes, treating them as one unit. Carry the reed over and around the rim to the inside of the basket, back out (the wrong side is now out) and over all five spokes, then under the handle bottom.

Continue to the left side by bringing the reed out and over all five spokes on the left, then under and around the rim to the inside, and back out again. The right side is now out. Weave back under the five spokes, then out and over the handle bottom again. You have completed one full row. See Step A on previous page.

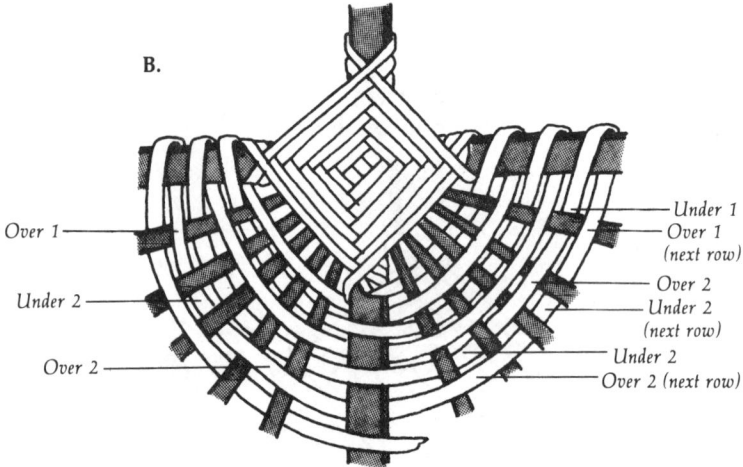

Continue this pattern for one more complete row, again ending at the handle bottom.

Now the pattern changes, as shown in Step B.

Continuing to the right, weave under two spokes, over the next two, under the last one, and then over and around the rim. Weave to the left now, over one spoke, under two, over two, and under the handle bottom. Continue this pattern on the left by weaving over two, under two, over one, under and around the rim. Then weave back, under one, over two, under two, and over the handle bottom. You have completed one row of this new pattern.

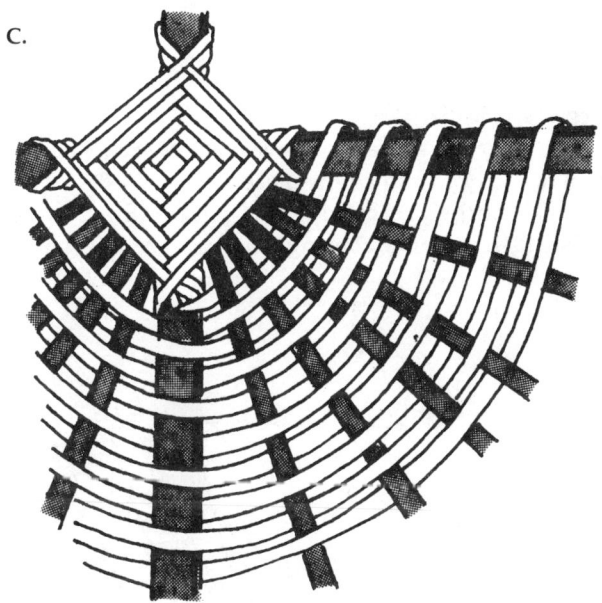

C.

Repeat this step so that you have woven two complete rows ending at the handle bottom.

Your weaving can now change to a simple over and under pattern, as shown in Step C.

You are starting on the outer side of the handle bottom. Weave under one spoke, over one spoke, under one, over one, under one, over and around the rim. Weave back down and over one spoke, under one, over one, under one, over one, and under the handle bottom.

Continue this pattern on the left side, weave over one, under one, over one, under one, over one, and under and around the rim. Weave back and go under one spoke, over one, under one, over one, under one, and over the handle bottom.

This pattern will be continued for the rest of the basket.

When the weaver is used up, secure it with a clothespin and repeat this breaking down process on the other side of the basket. The reason for alternating from side to side is that it's easier to make the basket more uniform in shape.

### Step 5. Piecing

You now have used up a weaver on each side of the basket. You're ready to add a new piece.

Soak another reed until it is pliable. Start on the side you finished first, remembering that you are alternating from one

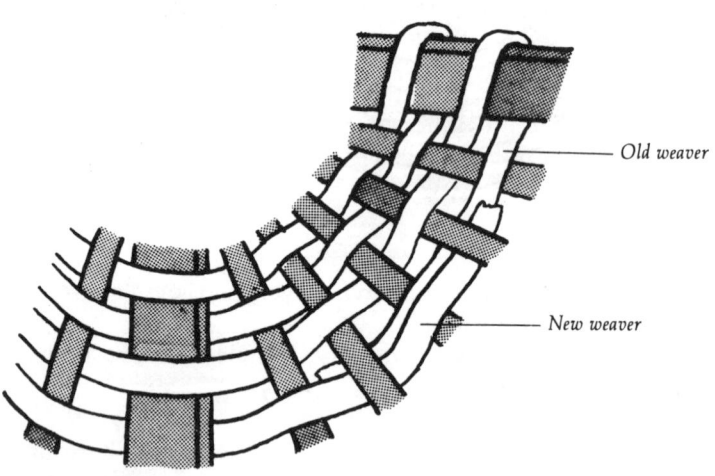

*Old weaver*

*New weaver*

side to the other. Place the new weaver right on top of the first one and overlap it by 3 or 4 inches. This should be done away from the rim. If the weaver ends near the rim, cut it back so the piecing stays in the middle. If the first weaver ended with the wrong side showing, lay the new weaver on top of the old one with the wrong side showing. Thus the pattern of rows alternating right and wrong sides will be continued.

The end of the new weaver can be tucked under a spoke or the handle bottom to hide it.

Proceed with the weaving as before by continuing with the new piece.

## Step 6. Completing the Weaving

Continue weaving from one side of the basket to the other. Do not, however, weave past the middle with either side of the weaving. If one section of weaving reaches the middle and there is some reed left, stop, clip the reed with a clothespin, then weave the other side until it reaches the middle.

When the weaving nears completion, the reed from each side is joined by overlapping one on top of the other, just as you did in piecing. You may need to cut one or both reeds to have them overlap by 3 or 4 inches, and not near the rim.

If you followed these directions exactly, the weaving pattern will be correct, so that the two reeds don't meet weaving over and under the same spoke.

But if you didn't and they do, you can do one of two things:

1. Gently push the weaving apart on each side (toward the rims) just enough to squeeze in another row of weaving and thus make the pattern correct.

2. If the space is too small for another row of weaving, take out the last uneven row. Then fill in the gap by gently pushing the weaving from each side toward the middle.

Finish by cutting any long ends, stray fibers, or wisps of reed. The basket should sit level. If it doesn't, soak it for a few minutes, then gently press down on the inside bottom, to form it so that it will sit level. Then I usually put a smooth round rock inside to weigh it down, and leave it to dry for a day or two.

## Step 7. The Handle

The handle can be left with the wooden hoop showing, or it can be covered in a variety of ways. Here are several ways:

**1. The Simple Wrap.**

Select a piece of 3/16-inch reed long enough so the handle can be wrapped without piecing. Soak it, then push one tapered end, right side down, into the space between the hoop and the top of the lashing. Fold the reed over and, with the right side now showing, begin to wrap rows of reed around the handle. Each row should be snug to the last one.

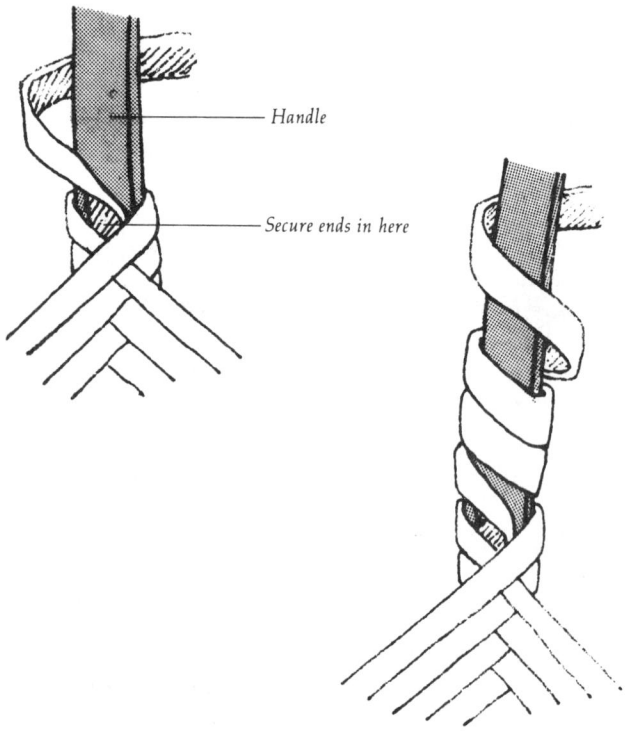

Continue wrapping around the handle to the other side. Cut the reed at an angle and short enough to push down into the space at the top of the lashing. An awl can be a great help in getting the end securely down inside the lashing.

## 2. The Woven Wrap.

Using the same wrap as in the simple wrap, a variety of patterns can be achieved by weaving over and under another strand of reed.

Secure both the soaked weaver and a length of thin reed, soaked, at the top of the lashing. This reed should be just a bit longer than the handle, it must reach from one lashing to the other.

Wrap the weaver once around the handle, going over the shorter reed. Next, pick up the reed and wrap the weaver under it. Continue this pattern, going over and under the reed, until all of the handle is covered. Secure the ends into the top of the lashing on the opposite side.

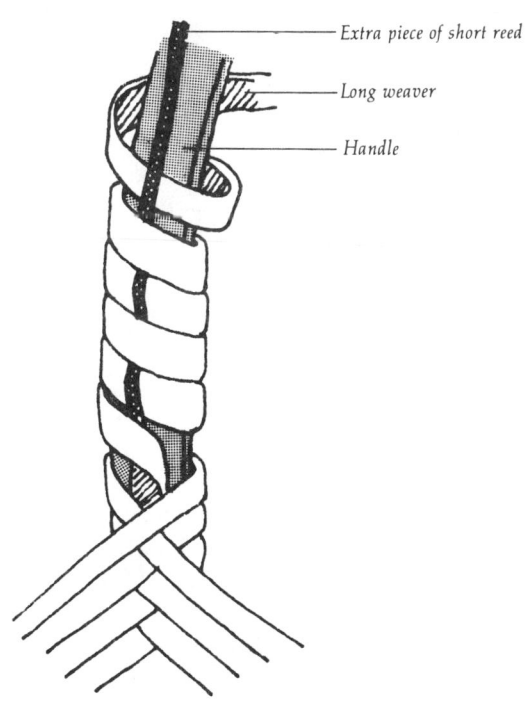

Extra piece of short reed
Long weaver
Handle

This pattern can be changed easily by weaving over or under the reed a different number of times. It could be over two, under two; or over two, under one; or over one, under two. A handle bigger than this one could be woven over and under three or more times.

Try changing the shape or color of the short reed. Or, with a wider handle, try adding two short reeds to weave through.

**3. Figure Eight Wrap.**

Cut two pieces of #7 round reed the length of the handle. Sharpen the ends, place one on each side of and parallel to the handle and tuck them inside the pockets behind the lashings.

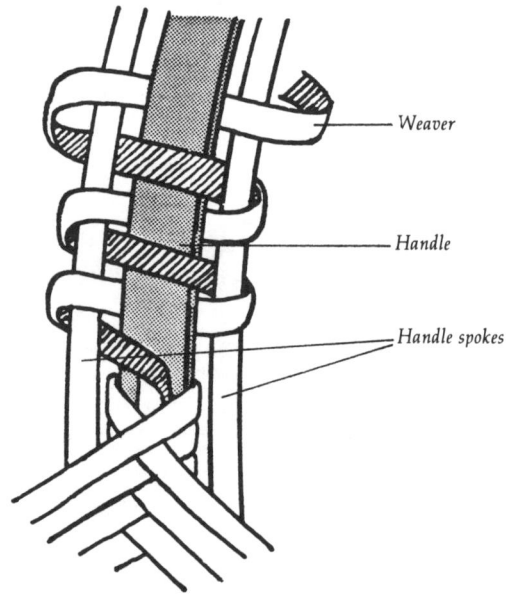

Select a lengthy weaver, soak it until it is pliable, then secure one end, wrong side down, in the space at the top of the lashing. Fold it over and weave it under and around one side spoke, under the handle, then up and around the other side spoke and over the handle. Continue weaving in this manner until the handle is completed. Secure the end of the weaver in the space at the top of the lashing on the opposite side.

# Dyes

Dyeing basket materials offers you a chance to use your imagination. It's a lot of fun. The flat and round reed, the spokes, and even some wild materials can be dyed. Or a whole basket can be dyed one color when it is completed. I prefer to dye my materials separately so that I can use more than one color in a basket.

The easiest and fastest method is to dye with packaged commercial fabric dye. Suppliers are listed on page 30.

One small package of dye (1⅛ ounces) will dye about a pound of reed. I mix the commercial packaged dye in our stainless steel kitchen sink, but a large, old pot or metal container can be used.

Mix according to package directions, using hot water right from the tap. Stir until well dissolved. Wet the reed before placing it in the dye bath. Leave the material in until it is the shade you want. Don't forget that it will look lighter when it dries.

I like to leave some reed in the dye for about 30 minutes, replace it with some that I leave in for 15 minutes, then replace that with some that I dye for just a few minutes. That gives me three shades of the same color.

Remove the reed from the dye bath with a stick or old wooden spoon, rinse it in clear water, and place it on lots of paper towels to drain. Then hang it to dry completely. I use our clothesline in the cellar for this, but any place outside in the shade will do.

When dyed reed is soaked later for weaving, some of the color may come out. Use separate soaking pans for each color.

If you have a large pot, you can dye a finished basket. First, try a test piece of reed to make certain the color is right. Then wet the basket, place it in the dye bath, and move it about with a stick. Take it out when it reaches the right shade, pat it with paper towels, and hang it up to dry. Leave some towels underneath to catch the drippings.

Some of my students have had excellent results using the stains sold for staining wood. Thin these with turpentine or mineral oil.

Acrylic or latex paint can also be thinned and applied directly to the basket with a brush. In each case, test with a small piece of reed to make certain the color is what you want.

You can also apply mineral or linseed oil to a basket. The oak basket hoops look especially beautiful when coated with oil.

If you're planning to use the basket for food, use a finish that is non-toxic, or leave the basket natural.

## Natural Dyes

Using dyes from natural materials requires time and patience, but is rewarding. The only dye I know of that does not call for a mordant (fixative) is black walnut hulls. The colors obtained from natural materials, without using a mordant, are not as longlasting nor as vivid, but paler and more subtle. I prefer them that way and feel better not using the many chemicals required in mordanting.

To use black walnut hulls:

Soak ½ pound of walnut hulls overnight in 3-4 gallons of water.

The next day boil the hulls in the water for an hour.

Let cool, then strain the dye through cheesecloth.

Wet the reed, and leave it in the dye until it is the desired shade.

To get a darker brown, try more hulls or less water.

This procedure can be used with coffee, tea, or any other natural materials.

# Variations

You now know how to weave a 10-inch basket, color it in different ways, and decorate its handle. It's time for us to experiment, to try new and different methods of weaving and variations on materials. Let's see what they are.

## Hoops

The basic basket can be changed in many ways by using a different size or shape of hoop. Round hoops come in sizes from 4 to 18 inches, and widths of ½ to ¾ inch. Oval hoops are available in several sizes. Try combining oval and round hoops, using one for the handle and the other for the rim. There are also "D" frames available for wall baskets and square frames for market baskets. All of these can be made using the same procedure as the basic basket.

Basket hoops, too, are offered in different woods — poplar, oak, hickory. Hard wood is preferred, but a beginner can start with less expensive plywood.

My favorite basket has wild grapevine for the hoops and spokes. I gather vines about ½ inch thick, peel off the bark, and twine the vine into a circle. Make two circles of the size desired, insert one inside the other, and follow the steps used in weaving the basic basket.

You can use thick vine for a large basket, thin vine for a small one. Because of the irregularities of the vine, I usually use a three-fold, instead of a four-fold lashing. (Instructions for this lashing are on pages 3 to 5.)

Other vines can be used, such as honeysuckle, wisteria, or whatever is native to your area. Even the thicker, purchased round reed can be twined into hoops and used to make especially attractive handles. So...experiment.

Whether you try a large, small, round, or oval basket, be sure to adjust your materials accordingly. By this I mean that for baskets smaller than the basic one, use narrower reed for weaving and a smaller size spoke. Just the opposite for a larger basket.

## Three-fold Lashing

A different type of lashing can be made to secure the basket hoops together. The three-fold lashing is a little easier, so if you have difficulty with the four-fold lashing, try this one. While I think the four-fold lashing is more secure and attractive, in some cases, such as with a grapevine basket or any basket without a handle, it is necessary to make a three-fold lashing. The following instructions are for a 10-inch basket.

Mark the hoops and set them in place. Soak a 3/16-inch weaver, then begin the lashing on one of the crossed sections of the hoops.

**Step A.** Place the reed, wrong side out, behind the handle bottom at point 1. Leave about an inch of the end to be tucked into the weaving as it progresses. At point 2, bring the reed up

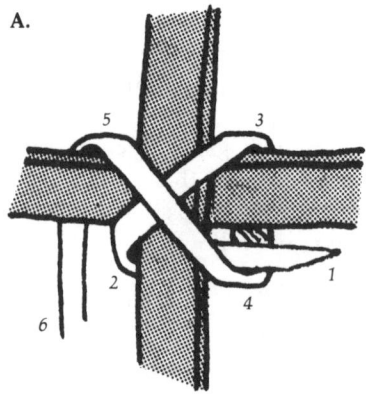

and across to the top of the rim on the right side to point 3. Bring the reed straight down behind the rim to point 4. Bring the reed up and across to the rim on the left side of point 5, then down behind the rim to point 6. This forms an X across the hoops, and only the right side of the reed should be seen.

**Step B.** At point 6, twist the reed so that it lies flat over the handle bottom with the right side showing. At point 7, twist again, and bring the reed under and around the rim to point 8, then back down to point 9. Twist and bring the reed under the handle bottom to point 10.

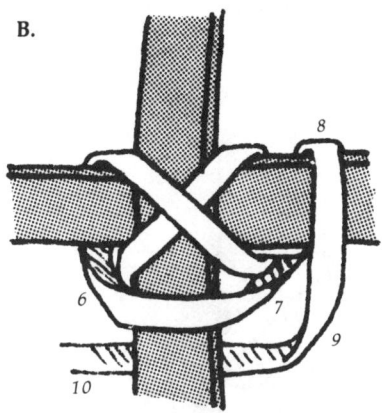

**Step C.** At point 10, twist the reed and bring it over and around the rim to point 11, then back down to point 12. Twist the reed and bring it over the handle bottom to point 13.

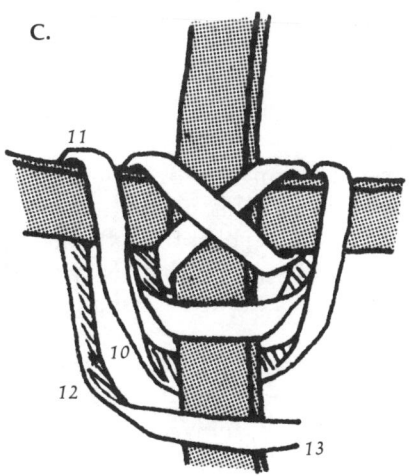

**Step D.** At point 13, twist and bring the reed under and around the rim to point 14, then down to point 15. Twist and bring the reed under the handle bottom to point 16. Continue in this manner for four or five rows. Note that the twisting in all cases is so that the right side of the reed will show. Stop at the handle bottom and secure the weaver with a clothespin. Repeat this much of the lashing on the other side of the basket.

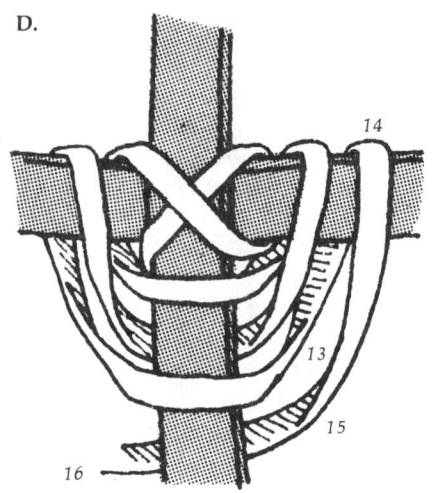

D.

### Placing the Spokes

With this method of lashing, the spokes have to be placed as the weaving progresses. At this point, two spokes should be added on each side. Cut four spokes from #7 round reed, making them 15½ inches long. Sharpen both ends of each spoke. Place one spoke in each of the spaces in the lashings, as shown.

Pick up the weaver where you secured it, and begin weaving over and under each spoke. Weave from rim to rim as in the weaving of the basic basket. After weaving two rows, secure the weaver with a clothespin at the handle bottom, and repeat this much on the other side of the basket.

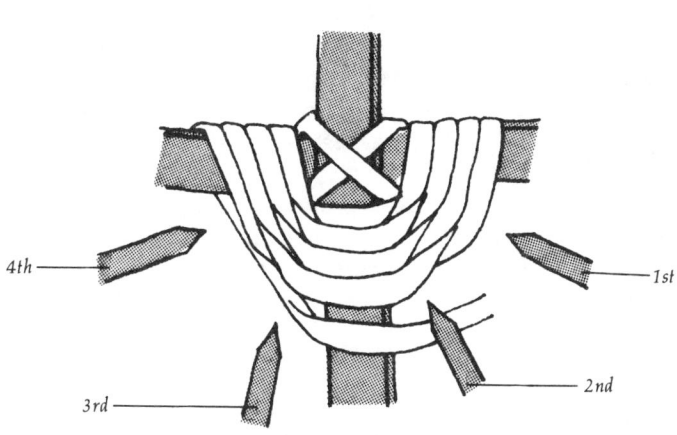

You will now add more spokes on each side of the basket. Cut and sharpen six spokes, three for each side. Four of them should be 13 inches long, two should be 15 inches long. Place them as shown below, with two 13-inch spokes under each side of the basket rims, two others on each side of the handle bottom, and the 15-inch spokes in the middle between the two original spokes. Push them into the weaving to secure them.

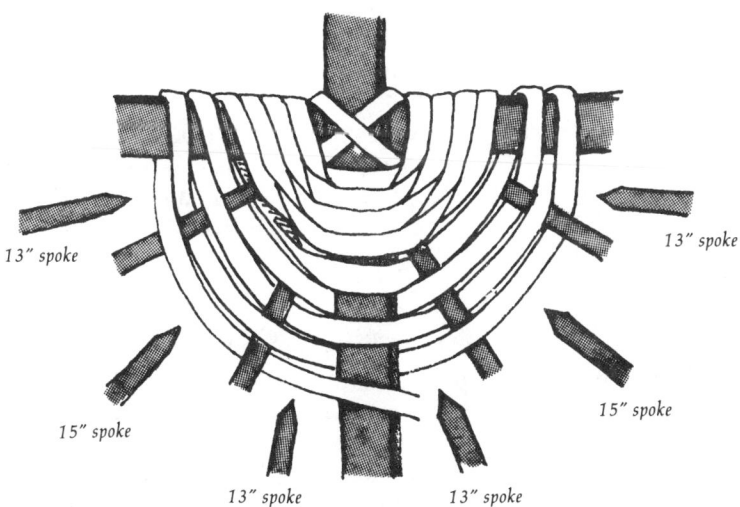

Starting again on top of the handle bottom, continue to weave over and under, going through all five spokes on each side of the basket, and around each rim.

When the reed is used up, repeat the weaving on the other side, until that weaver is used up. If you are delayed in doing all of this and the reed becomes too dry for weaving, soak what remains while holding the basket close to the surface of the water.

Continue the weaving, piecing, and finishing as described for the basic basket. For a variation, however, you can complete an equal number of rows on each side with the 3/16-inch reed, then switch to ¼-inch reed, doing the piecing for this at the handle bottom.

## Spokes

Spokes form the framework and determine the shape of the basket bottom. By varying their length and placement, spokes can be used to construct round baskets, egg-shaped baskets, or any variation in between. As you become more familiar with the basic principles of basket-weaving, you will be able to make a shape that pleases your eye without using any measurements.

The thickness or size of the spokes must vary according to the size of the basket. Here is a table of the spoke sizes that go best with various sizes of baskets.

| ROUND REED | MM SIZE* | HOOP SIZE |
|---|---|---|
| #4 round reed | 2¾ | 4-inch or smaller basket |
| #5 round reed | 3¼ | 6-inch or 8-inch basket |
| #6 round reed | 4½ | 8-inch or 10-inch basket |
| #7 round reed | 5 | 10-inch or 12-inch basket |
| #8 round reed | 5¾ | 12-inch or 14-inch basket |

*The MM (millimeter) size differs among many suppliers. Check when ordering.

If you make a basket smaller than the 10-inch basic basket, you will need fewer than ten spokes — and a bigger basket will require more than ten spokes.

On the larger baskets, since the pocket of the lashing won't hold more than five spokes on each side, the extra spokes must be added after the weaving has started. Here's how we do it.

## Adding Extra Spokes

With larger baskets the space between spokes shouldn't be more than 1½ inches. If it is, extra spokes must be added. To add spokes, complete weaving the same number of rows on each side of the basket. Measure the length of the still-exposed areas of the other spokes, add about 2 inches to this length, and cut spokes that length. Sharpen both ends of the spokes, then insert them as shown below.

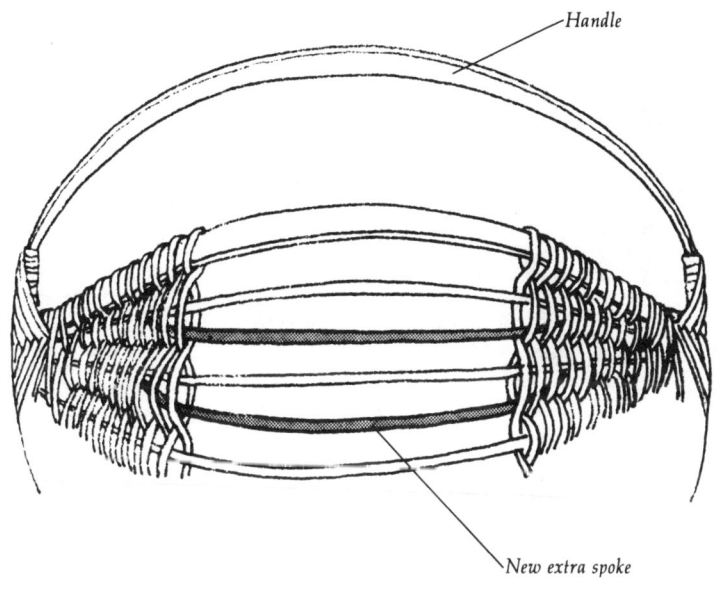

You will, of course, add spokes in pairs, two on each side of the basket. The weaving then continues by including the additional spokes.

For a variation on any basket, try placing extra spokes on top of the rim. They can be longer than the rim, to form a wide ridge or lip on the basket, or they can be smaller, to close in the opening of the basket.

Tuck the spokes into the pocket of the lashing, on top of the rim.

Weaving and other procedures are unchanged. Just continue each row of weaving past the rim and over the extra spokes. Treat the last spoke as you do the rim in the basic basket. Bend the weaver around it and continue weaving back down.

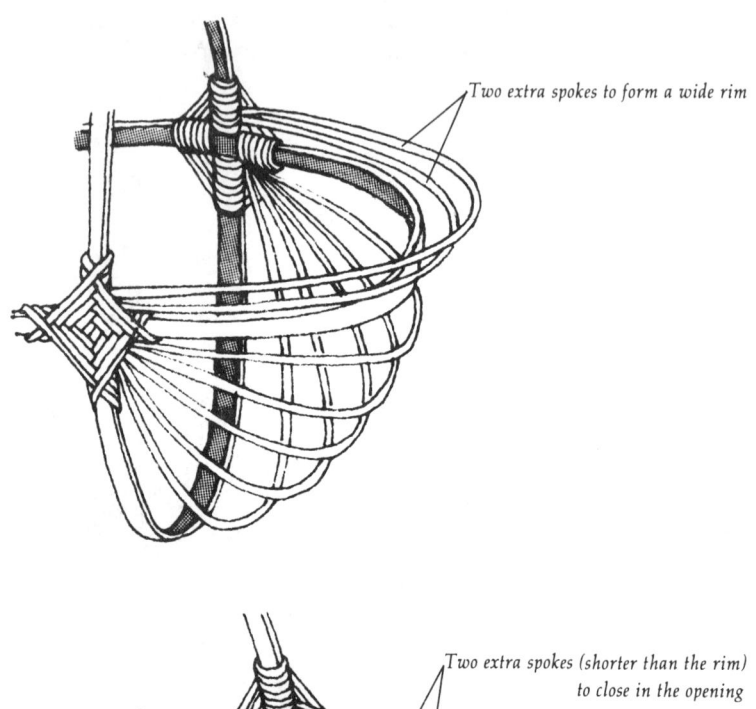

Two extra spokes to form a wide rim

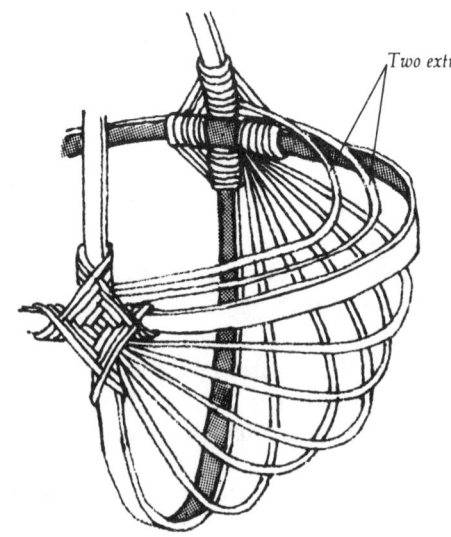

Two extra spokes (shorter than the rim) to close in the opening

# Egg Baskets

An egg basket can be made by following the earlier instructions for making the basic basket. The one difference is that the spokes must be of different lengths.

Here are the lengths of the spokes you will need for a 10-inch egg basket:

4 spokes 15½ inches long
4 spokes 16 inches long
2 spokes 16½ inches long

Extra spokes, added after the weaving measures 3 inches on each side:

4 spokes 11½ inches long
2 spokes 10½ inches long
2 spokes 12½ inches long

The diagram shows the pattern of the spokes on one side of the basket. Repeat the pattern on the other side.

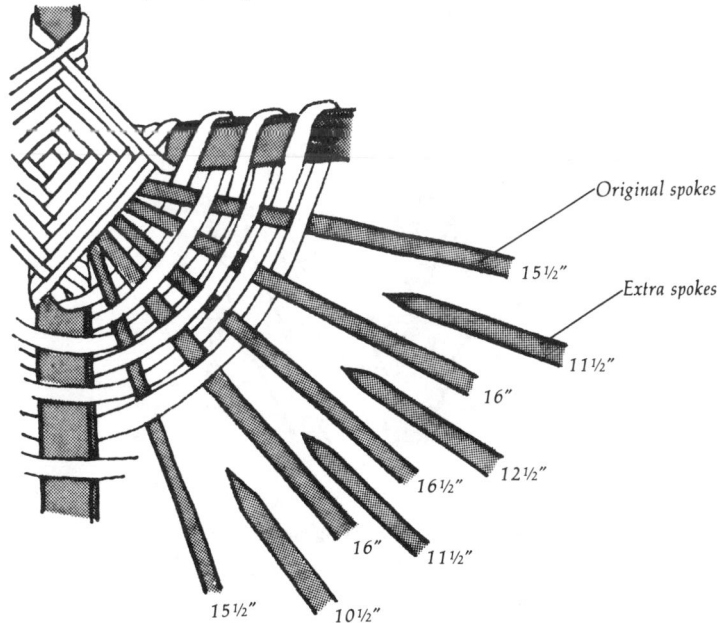

Because of the shape of the egg basket, the weaving will completely fill the rim, and cover the handle bottom, while the middle sections remain unwoven.

This space can be filled in by continuing with a weaver you are already using, or starting a new one, overlapping the earlier weaver at the handle bottom. Weave over and under in the usual manner, until you reach the first or second spoke nearest the rim. Bend the weaver over the spoke, as you would at the rim, and continue weaving to the other side. Again, bend the reed over the first or second spoke near the rim and weave all the way back within one or two spokes of the previous bend. Weave around that spoke, and back down to within one or two spokes of the previous bend on the other side.

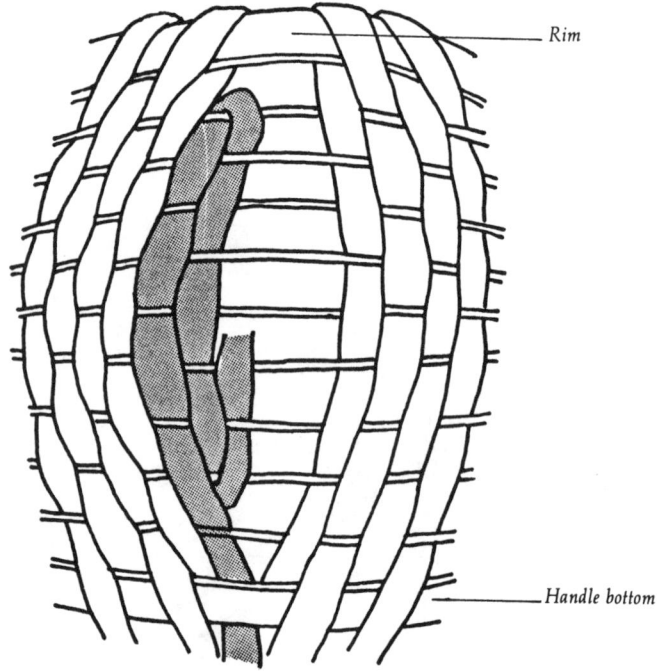

Continue weaving through progressively fewer spokes until you have reached the widest part of the space. Then reverse the process by increasing the number of spokes you weave over until the area is completely filled in.

Treat each unwoven space in the same manner, using this step-like procedure. With an egg basket of this size, you may have to weave only a few rows to fill in the middle.

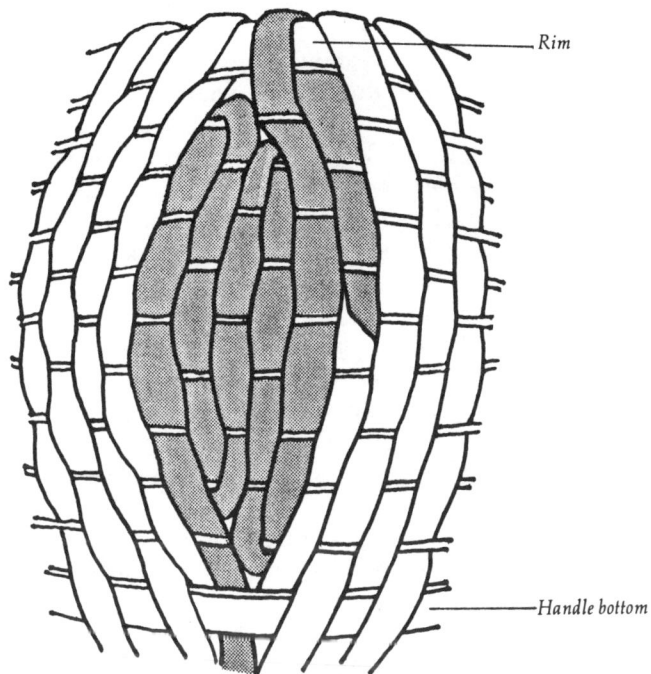

## Weaving Variations

In hoop-constructed basketry, the weaving pattern remains constant, but many variations can be achieved by using different weaving materials. In this way you can add color, texture, and interest.

Flat reed used for weaving comes in widths from 3/16 to 1 inch. Try weaving with different widths. Be sure to keep the width of the reed proportional to the basket size — too wide a reed, for example, will look cumbersome in a small basket.

It is also possible to weave with some of the small, round reed. It is available in sizes from #0 (1¼ MM size) to #17 (15¾ MM). The thicker round reed, from about #5 up, is primarily used for spokes. I like to weave with round reed at the beginning of the weaving. The lashing can also be done in #2 round reed.

Add interest by weaving in some wild materials. Your choices include thin vines, strips of bark, cattail leaves, and cornhusks. Even twine, seagrass, and wool fabric strips can be used. Experiment with these and others.

As for colored reed, the sky is the limit. Dye your own and make rows of various colors.

Be certain, whenever changing colors or weaving materials, to do the piecing at the handle bottom. Each new row should be started at that central point.

# Exterior Weaving

When the basket is completed, extra weaving, usually in a contrasting color, can be done along the outside of the rim and the handle bottom.

Soak a piece of narrow reed until it is pliable. Insert one tapered end into the side of the lashing, then weave over and under each piece of reed along the rim. When the weaving reaches the other side, cut the end and slide it into the side of the other lashing. The next row of weaving should be done just below the first row. Alternate the weaving so that the second reed goes under where the first reed went over.

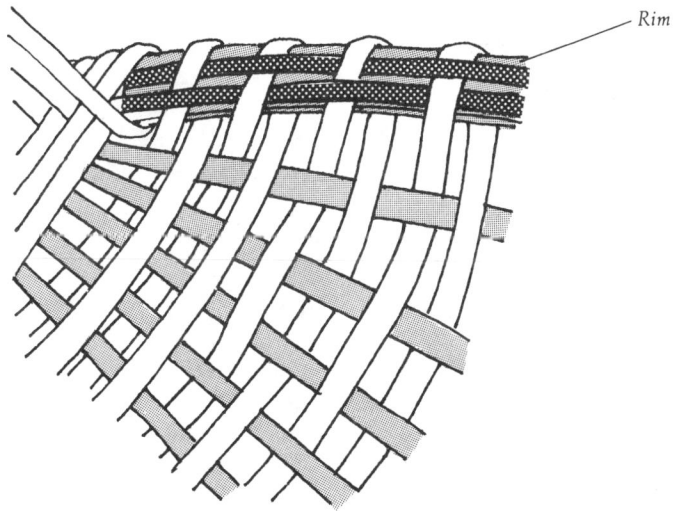

Rim

Repeat this exterior weaving on the other half of the rim. A knife or slender tool, such as a small screwdriver, is very helpful for gently lifting up the reed so the weaver can slide under it. Usually, with a ¾-inch hoop, only two rows of exterior weaving can be done along the rim. It will, of course, depend on the width of the reed you are using.

There is usually enough room along the handle bottom to fit three rows of exterior weaving. Insert the tapered end of the weaver into the bottom of the lashing, weave around to the other side, cut, and secure the other end into the bottom of the lashing on that side. Repeat for two more rows, making sure that the weaving pattern is the opposite of the first row. I sometimes like to use a different color in the middle row and repeat that color in the handle.

## SOURCES OF SUPPLIES AND TOOLS

Bamboo and Rattan Works, Inc.
470 Oberlin Ave. South
Lakewood, NJ 08701-6997

Connecticut Cane and Reed Co.
PO Box 1276
Manchester, CT 06040

The H.H. Perkins Co.
10 S. Bradley Rd.
Woodbridge, CT 06525

Cane and Basket Supply Co.
1283 S. Cochran Ave.
Los Angeles, CA 90019

Peerless Rattan
22 Lake Ave., Box 636
Yonkers, NY 10701

Sax Arts and Crafts
PO Box 2002
Milwaukee, WI 53201

## NATURAL DYE MATERIALS

The Mariposa Tree, Inc.
PO Box 366, Stapleton,
Staten Island, NY 10340
(Offers commercial dyes in
83 colors)

Country Herbs
Route 7
Stockbridge, MA 01262

## CHEMICAL DYE COMPANIES

Pro Chemical and Dye, Inc.
PO Box 14
Somerset, MA 02726

FabDec Co.
3553 Old Post Rd.
San Angelo, TX 76904

# BASKET KITS

Indian Hill Collection
346 Main Ave.
PO Box 3767
Norwalk, CT 06851

Ozark Oak Basket Kits
#1 Park Dr.
Roxana, IL 62084

Maryanne Gillooly
Wildwood Basketry
RD 2, Box 156
Great Barrington, MA 01230
Sells two kits, a 10-inch melon kit for $13.95, and a 10-inch egg basket kit for $15.95, postage paid. For $1.50 extra, these kits are available in wine red, forest green, Colonial blue or Smoky brown. Massachusetts residents should add 5 percent sales tax.

Basketry Studio A
PO Box 300
West Barnstable, MA 12668

River Baskets
1321 Linda St., Dept. 10
Rocky River, OH 44116

Other sources of supplies:
*(mostly exotic materials)*

Basket Beginnings
3001 Ross Ave. #3 (95124)
P.O. Box 24815
San Jose, Ca. 95154-4815

Tint & Splint Basketry
29529 Ford Rd.
Garden City, Mich. 48135

The Hen's Tooth 971-8363
6225 Cockspur Drive
Alexandria, Va. 22310

Coastal Flowering Plants
P.O. Box 809
Pahoa, Hawaii 96778

Wovenware
3465 Edgewater Drive
Orlando, Fla. 32804

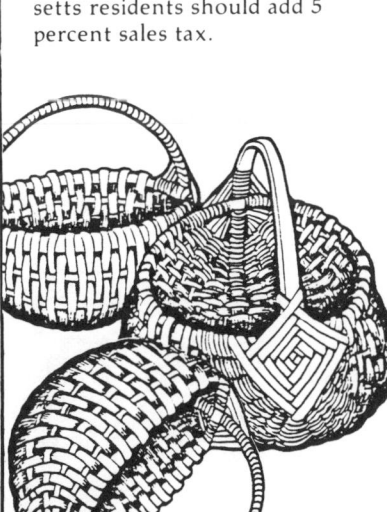